RHYME CRAFT

Derbyshire & Nottinghamshire Poets

Edited By Julie Macdonald

First published in Great Britain in 2018 by:

Young Writers

Young Writers
Remus House
Coltsfoot Drive
Peterborough
PE2 9BF
Telephone: 01733 890066
Website: www.youngwriters.co.uk

FOREWORD

Young Writers was established in 1991, dedicated to encouraging reading and creative writing in young people. Our nationwide writing initiatives are designed to inspire ideas and give pupils the incentive to write, and in turn develop literacy skills and confidence, whilst participating in a fun, imaginative activity.

Few things are more encouraging for the aspiring writer than seeing their own work in print, so we are proud that our anthologies are able to give young authors this unique sense of confidence and pride in their abilities.

For our latest competition, Rhymecraft, primary school pupils were asked to enter a land of poetry where they used poetic techniques such as rhyme, simile and alliteration to bring their ideas to life. The result is an entertaining and imaginative anthology which will make a charming keepsake for years to come.

Each poem showcases the creativity and talent of these budding new writers as they learn the skills of writing, and we hope you are as entertained by them as we are.

CONTENTS

Fritchley CE (A) Primary School, Fritchley

Amy-Leigh Hunt (7)	47
Oliver Toplis (7)	48
Harriet Clarke (9)	49
Sam Lynam (8)	50
Matilda Deans (9)	51
Danielle Wade (8)	52
Joe Allen (8)	53

Howitt Primary School, Heanor

Connie Abbott (11)	54
James Tyler (7)	55
Tymoteusz Krzyzanowski (11)	56
Lilly-Anne Iafrate (7)	57

Larkfields Junior School, Nuthall

Theo William Stokes (8)	58
Aaron Curtis (10)	59
Thomas Wood (10)	60

Middleton Community Primary School, Middleton By Wirksworth

Ava Spencer (9)	61
Shannon Iris Rose Harrison	62
Hailie Croll (10)	63
Hannah Fretter (11)	64
Oliver Love (11)	65
Breidi Megan Moran (8)	66

Normanton House School, Derby

Zaynah Khan (11)	67
Hafsa Bhatti (9)	68
Ayesha Ahmed (11)	70
Halimah Hussain	71
Sumaiyah Naseer (10)	72
Abdul Rahman Basit (11)	73
M Ibrahim Naseer (8)	74
Zayan Bashir (10)	75
Ishaaq Naeem (11)	76

Hasan Malik (9)	77
Yusrah Khandakar (9)	78
Musab Asir (9)	79
Muhammad Umar Hussain (11)	80
Hafsa Bint-Umran (8)	81
Hassan Mahmood (10)	82
Ayisha Halima Qureshi (11)	83
M Ahmed Ahmed (9)	84
Noor Hussain	85
Uzair Abid (8)	86
Hamza Mahmood (7)	87

North Wheatley Primary School, South Wheatley

Madeleine Bambridge (11)	88
Callum Dale (10)	89
Freya Rose North (11)	90
Dominic Newby (9)	92
Owen Dale (10)	93
Scarlett Wilkinson (9)	94
Neve Lily Baker (11)	95
Ben Launders (10)	96
Nicole Marie Cocksedge (11)	97
Katie McKay (10)	98
Ella Worden (10)	99

S. Anselm's School, Bakewell

Ruby Coco Brailich (9)	100
Holly Kilner (9)	101
Isabella Mayson (9)	102

Southglade Primary School, Bestwood Park

Isabelle Bowen (10)	103
Damian Raynor (10)	104

St Edward's Catholic Academy, Swadlincote

Alexis Summer Bode (8)	105
Ruby Carpenter (8)	106
Ethan Hanif Edmonds (9)	107
Lilly Cox (8)	108
Megan Rose Coope (9)	109
Evan Shipley (9)	110
Sonnie Mercer (8)	111
Jack Freeman (9)	112
Autumn Warner (9)	113
Isabel Meikle (9)	114
Keenan Baldwin (9)	115
Ethan Kelly (9)	116
Sam Sellers (9)	117
Gabriella Jane Bellafronte (9)	118
Isabelle-Mollie Flanagan-Nicholls (9)	119
George Alexander Radley (9)	120
Connie Denning (8)	121
Myles Mondesir (8)	122
Cerise Joyce Cotton (8)	123
Amelie Lewek (8)	124
Domink Sidorczuk (9)	125
Lewis Rayson (8)	126
Aimee-Leigh Maisie Randle (9)	127
Evangelene Puthussery (9)	128

St Giles CE Primary School, Matlock

Eva Brailsford (8)	129
Maisey Diveney-Moffat (8)	130
Emily Kerry (9)	132
Lila Staley (8)	134
Daisy Bridger (7)	135
Sienna Gulliford (8)	136
Hannah Katherine Smith (7)	137
Andrew Slater (8)	138
Ellis Mousley (8)	139
Jayleize Scoffins (9)	140
Jackell Scoffins (8)	141
Jolie Haywood (8)	142

Michael Gibson (9)	143
Summer Oldfield (7)	144
Aidan Woodward (7)	145

St Luke's CE Primary School, Shireoaks

John-Phil Cunningham (9)	146
Nina Davide (8)	147
Sophie Robley (9)	148
Ava Keyworth (8)	149
Finlay McEvoy (8)	150
Devan Singh Gill (8)	151
Iona Watson (8)	152
Millie Grace Pickering (8)	153
Jessica Kate Harrison (9)	154
Abbi Hopkinson (8)	155

The Linnet Independent Learning Centre, Castle Gresley

Cameron Watkins (11)	156
Ryan Elliott (11)	157

Wessington Primary School, Wessington

Nicole Batchford (9)	158
Archie Taylor (8)	159
Summer Edge	160
Eden Kunica (8)	161
Sam Brown (8)	162
Jasper Marshall (9)	163
Eleanor Hayes (8)	164
Amber-Louise Buckely (9)	165
Oliver Davis (8)	166
Louis McPherson (9)	167
William Race Beckett (7)	168

Wirksworth Junior School, Wirksworth

Freya Lilian Wilson (8)	169
Lyla Hunt (8)	170
Caitlin Butler (7)	171

THE POEMS

Candy Land

Candy Land is a wonderful place.
You can solve your case.
The cakes are baked.
The lollipop is burning.
The clock is turning.

The roses smell so sweet.
You can eat the wheat.
The rain is Skittles.
They are very little.
It all tastes so good.

Rubie Weller (12)
Alfreton Park Community Special School, Alfreton

Candy World

Candy is so good
It gets in your blood
It's the sweetest place to be
Candy trees are free
There are candy canes and lollipops
When you see the treasure chest, you must stop
The chest is full of candy
The floor is sandy
In Candy World.

Chloe Carter (15)

Alfreton Park Community Special School, Alfreton

Atlantis

I saw the castle with my two eyes
I could taste the air as I went to the castle
When I went into the castle, I smelt power
Upon touching the crown
I felt so energetic
From behind me I heard
The sound of footsteps, *stomp, stomp, stomp.*

Jamie Lee Fox (13)
Alfreton Park Community Special School, Alfreton

Underwater

The sea is blue
You can come too
It has sea creatures in
You can ride on top of a dolphin
You will find treasure
At the bottom of the sea
To open up the treasure
You will need a key.

Logan Harwood (10)

Alfreton Park Community Special School, Alfreton

Happy Candy Lands

I can taste the delicious lollipop candy
I smell sweet candy
I see chocolate, Skittles and lollipops
I hear raining chocolate balls
I touch marshmallow on the ground
It feels sticky!

Jake Lambert (11)
Alfreton Park Community Special School, Alfreton

Candy Land

C andy Land is great
A t the candy house, you can have a...
N ice day out with candy animals
D elicious candy treats
Y ou can have fun there.

Peter Green (7)

Alfreton Park Community Special School, Alfreton

Food Land

H ere at Food Land
A pples are on top of houses
P eople eat macaroni cheese
P lanes take you up to the bowling alley
Y ou can have fun!

Lewis Leslie Williamson (7)

Alfreton Park Community Special School, Alfreton

Food Land

My food land is a fun land.
I taste hot and cold food.
I smell my favourite food in the air.
I hear loud people cheering and laughing.
I see food everywhere.

Kevin Burt (12)
Alfreton Park Community Special School, Alfreton

Dinosaur Land

In Dinosaur Land everything is grand.
Lemonade tastes good, not like wood.
The river is green and no trees can be seen.
The sky is blue, like a dinosaur's poo.
Pirates live here and can be seen drinking beer.
The dinosaur is green and the biggest I've
ever seen.
The lava here is red and has killed many dead.
Sweets are their food, which puts the dinosaurs in
a good mood.
Come to this place and make it your base.

Jamie Dutch (9)
Bakewell Methodist Junior School, Bakewell

Running Land

R unning makes you fit,
U nder and over obstacles,
N ever slowing down,
N ever giving up,
I will always try my best,
N ow let's go faster!
G oing as fast as a cheetah.

L et's get into place,
A re you ready?
N ow let the race commence!
D id you win?

Alex Barks (9)

Bakewell Methodist Junior School, Bakewell

My World Of Rugby!

R acing and mauling to win the ball.
U sing your peripheral vision.
G athering for a team talk before the game.
B eing with your friends.
Y -lining to drag the opposition.

M anipulating the defender.
A ttacking.
T actics.
C atching and passing.
H aving fun together.

Max Wood (9)
Bakewell Methodist Junior School, Bakewell

Sporty Adventure Land

S uper exciting fun for you and your friends.

P osition your players in any formation.

O r play an epic one vs one.

R eplay matches again and again.

T ry to win the football league.

S neak a peek at this sporty adventure land!

Angus Oliver (10)

Bakewell Methodist Junior School, Bakewell

The Haunted Pair

Down in the valley, a house lies alone,
Its windows are boarded, its chimney all stone,
But sometimes the door will just open a crack,
To let you see the top of a pointed witch's hat,
We hear cackles upon cackles come from
this shack,
Not to mention the miaowing that comes from
a cat,
Its eyes emerald green, its fur sleek and black,
There's no doubt that this animal is a cat.
No one dare enter through the doors,
No one wants to hear the ferocious cat's paws,
Your heart skips a beat when you see its
sharp claws,
The chimney blows smoke into the cold winter air,
There's no doubt that this is a troublesome pair!

Annabelle Cormican (10)
Barlborough Hall School, Barlborough

Candy Land

Just drop your worries, grab my hand,
Let's leave today for Candy Land,
Where problems fade and float away.

Like butterflies upon the breeze,
It's there you'll find the chocolate road,
That leads you to the crystal-blue sea
Which fizzes and bubbles, then explodes.

As teams of fish swim around a ribbon candy reef,
We'll take our time, then on a whim,
Sail on a giant spearmint leaf.

Next, let's go to Cookie City,
Where gummy frogs lurk in the chocolate river,
And let's jump on a cookie,
Floating on some milk,
That will take us back home.

Millie Grace Hatfield (9)
Barlborough Hall School, Barlborough

Music Land

There is a place where you can go,
Where bright rainbows shimmer in the sky,
Music Land is bright and festive,
Always here to brighten your day,
The houses are tall and hot pink,
The fact that this land is festive all year round,
Makes nothing ever sad, from high up to the
ground.

When you see the sign that says: *Singing
Harmony*,
Over the crystal-clear stream,
It makes you think of a fairy-tale dream,
So in this land, you will find,
Nobody is ever left behind.

Phoebe Rose Dayson (8)
Barlborough Hall School, Barlborough

Sweets, Sweets, Sweets

In this place all you can see
Are sweets, sweets, sweets,
There is no wheat,
All you can eat is sweets,
The rainbow is flavoured chocolate,
There are trees made out of doughnuts.

The animals are all gummy,
But they make your tummy rumble,
Strawberries, gummy mushrooms
And don't forget the lollipops

Clouds are made out of marshmallow,
And they are all yellow,
It's the best place in the world,
I love my land,
Because it's full of candy!

Sophia Brooke Henshaw (9)
Barlborough Hall School, Barlborough

Fairy Tale Land

Goldilocks sleeps in Baby Bear's bed,
Down in the forest is Little Red,
Rapunzel is watching out of her tower,
The evil witch of the east has lost her power,
Nemo jumps out of the sea,
The Mad Hatter drinks some crazy tea.

Sleeping Beauty wants to wake,
She wants a kiss from a prince, not a piece of cake,
Tinker Bell is flying in the sky,
Hansel and Gretel are making a pie,
I love this fairy tale land of mine,
But now it's time to finish my rhyme.

Tess Wilson (9)
Barlborough Hall School, Barlborough

Unicorn Land

U p in the clouds,

N ear Neverland,

I s a place,

C laustrophobically full of unicorns,

O h how the music plays so loud,

R eally beautiful thick, colourful manes,

N ever ever sadness.

L ittle baby unicorn is just growing her horn,

A s the majestic queen unicorn rules the land,

N ear the palace lives an evil queen unicorn,

D o not go near her, she will ruin your dreams.

Neev Chung (10)

Barlborough Hall School, Barlborough

Floating Lands

Some are connected with chains,
Welcome to the floating lands!

In the world of the skies,
Where everyone flies,
There are many dragons,
And very few wagons.

With advanced technology,
And incredible geology,
Chains that hold the islands together,
Will hold forever.

The wings in the skies,
Conquers and flies,
With the breath of flame,
It's not fair game.

Zak Brooks (10)
Barlborough Hall School, Barlborough

Magic Land

Far, far away in a magical land,
Where the green grass glitters,
Like the starry, sparkly sky,
The sky shines as bright as the sun.

Fairies fly across the sky,
And wizards cast a spell,
Unicorns ride across the rainbow road.

Pixies dance across the night sky,
Where butterflies fly,
I wish I could go there one day,
Up in the clouds, that's where I will play.

Evie Booth (8)
Barlborough Hall School, Barlborough

Parallel Lands

T he twin lands are
W onderful and incredible
I n your nightmares you visit them
N ightmare and Miserable Land.

L ovely Normal Land is better and more
A mazing than
N ightmare Land, and in your
D reams you visit the lovely, bright land
S o come and visit our lands in your dreams!

Nikhil Hari Davies (10)
Barlborough Hall School, Barlborough

Candy Land

In this land is a flowing chocolate river,
The bonbons are so sour, they make you shiver,
There is a ginormous castle made of gum,
If you lick the walls, it will make you go yum yum.

When you walk along the path of Skittles,
You will have to do a load of riddles,
On your journey you will see,
Candy growing on trees planted just for me!

Erin Tara Gent (9)
Barlborough Hall School, Barlborough

Sweet Candy Land

Jelly beans, jelly beans on the side,
Jelly beans, jelly beans stretched out wide.

Every biscuit house,
Has a tiny chocolate mouse.

The chimneys are made of cupcakes,
That everybody makes.

But everything is pretty,
Especially in Candy City.

So come and visit this place,
Where you can stuff your face!

Isla Park (8)
Barlborough Hall School, Barlborough

Enchanted Forest

Deep down in my Enchanted Forest...
I see glowing lanterns in the trees,
Beautiful butterflies in the sky,
I feel a lovely, windy breeze,
And the sweet smell of pie.

There's a crystal-blue lake,
With an enchanted wishing well,
Lots of wishes you can make,
With one supernatural spell!

Megan Keira Sanderson (9)
Barlborough Hall School, Barlborough

Winter Wonderland

The rides are fun but there's no sun.
Winter Wonderland is freezing and
sometimes breezy.
The place is cool but there's no pool.
You have to wear a coat if you sail a boat.
It's really cold and all the money is old.
In Winter Wonderland, there's no bugs.
Neither do they have rugs.
Winter Wonderland is the best.
You have to wear a vest.
The ice is hard.
You don't have a backyard.
I love Winter Wonderland!

Hana Sharif (9)
Fig Tree Primary School, Hyson Green

Candy Land

Candy Land is so yummy
Everything is colourful
And I don't get black teeth
It's always sunny
The food is not raw
I can wish for anything I want
When it's my birthday
Everyone celebrates
With sweets and more
When I am sad or upset
The candy cheers me up
I had a rest in my gingerbread house
It has a chocolate chimney
It rains chocolate drops
I love Candy Land!

Sara Fatima Hussain (8)
Fig Tree Primary School, Hyson Green

Meep City

M y city is big, like a giant ball in the sky

E veryone is happy in my city because everyone is friends

E veryone has a cute pet called Meep

P eek in the shop, it's open every day and night

C ity is big, no sadness around

I n pizza shops, everything is free

T o be a VIP, pay 3p

Y es, come to Meep City!

Luqman Hamed (8)

Fig Tree Primary School, Hyson Green

Creative Candy Land

My Candy Land doesn't need tasting
The air is really sweet
My Candy Land has birds that tweet
Everything is different, like fruit is bad for you
But sweets are so healthy
My Candy Land isn't smelly
It's like strawberry sweets, yum!
My Candy Land is so sugary
And the best part is the raspberry gum.
My Candy Land is the best!

Huriya Khan (8)
Fig Tree Primary School, Hyson Green

Science World

S cience Land is fun

'C ause you get to invent

I n Science World you get to invent anything

E verybody can be scientists if they want

N obody can say that there are rules because there aren't

C an you believe there are no rules?!

E veryone needs to try science!

Ibrahim Sageer (8)

Fig Tree Primary School, Hyson Green

Candy Land

My Candy Land is scrumptious
It's even delicious
There's even a lollipop sunshine
I can even see some gummy wine!

My house is made of gingerbread
The chocolate river is spread
There's a castle made of jelly
That I showed to Kelly!

That's my world!

Mehnaz Rashid (8)
Fig Tree Primary School, Hyson Green

Sports Land

I woke up
I heard football fans
Cheering for Man City
Because they scored
I smelt chips and pizza
I saw Messi score a goal
I tasted the chips
I touched the stadium
It was cool
I love Sports Land!

Abdullah Saqib (8)
Fig Tree Primary School, Hyson Green

Music Land

My land is fun
My land is colourful
My land is full of toys and drama
My land is cool
Because there is no school
My land is made of music
My land is funny!

Furqan Hamed (8)
Fig Tree Primary School, Hyson Green

Candy Land

In Candy Land
Everything is grand
It is all sweet
With no meat
I love candy
It makes me handy
It is very yummy
In my tummy.
I love Candy Land!

Umme-Hanee I (8)
Fig Tree Primary School, Hyson Green

Candy Kingdom

Everything is edible in my world...

I hear cupcake cars roaring along the road,
I see children playing on the candy cane park
I smell the chocolate river as it goes under the
strawberry pencil bridge,
I taste freshly baked cookies,
I touch the doorknob of my gingerbread house,
I love sweets!

Eleanor Carr (10)
Firfield Primary School, Breaston

Friends Forever And Always

F orever and always

R espect you

I nclude you

E ncourage you all the way

N eed you

D eserve you.

Abigail Caswell (9)

Firfield Primary School, Breaston

Land Of Myths

The unicorn's horn glistens golden in the sunlight.
Her flowing mane is as soft as silk.
Her fur is as white as milk.
Her voice echoes around the earth.
Her song, more beautiful than any bird.

The mermaids swim around peacefully.
Their tails are rainbow-coloured and long.
The water flows all around them.
Glistening blueish, silver and gold.

Phoenix's wings shine bright in the sky.
Her feathers are yellow and red.
Her beak's the shape of an ice cream cone.
Her feet are fiery twigs.
Her eyes are bright.

The fairies sit peacefully on the toadstools.
Their wings flutter gracefully as they sing their fairy
songs.

Their dainty feet float above the ground.
Their hair bouncing upon their heads.

I believe in them all!

Imogen Pot (9)
FitzHerbert CE Primary School, Fenny Bentley

Doodle Land

I will doodle
You a poodle
And colour it pink
The next doodle I draw
Will make me think.

I draw a square pig
And he likes to dig
I draw an oval rabbit
Eating is his habit.

I draw a colourful hen
He lives in a swirly pen
I draw a stretchy dog
He lives with a frog.

I draw a rainbow cat
He gets chased by a rat
I draw a pet mouse
He lives in a massive house.

This land is confusing
But also amusing
I love doodling!

Lily May Bull (9)
FitzHerbert CE Primary School, Fenny Bentley

Season Land

Winter's bright with snow,
As you may know,
Ice is on the lake,
Allowing us to skate.

Spring is finally here,
And summer's very near,
Lambs go out to play,
In the middle of the day.

Summer means school holiday,
When all day we can play,
I feel the summer air,
Brushing in my hair.

Autumn leaves fly down,
And cover the town,
The animals hide away,
As winter's on the way.

Edie Miller (8)

FitzHerbert CE Primary School, Fenny Bentley

What Am I?

I live in a land of danger,
But mankind can't beat us,
We protect our eggs,
But not all of us win.

We fight for our survival,
Until the end of the world,
Our roar is like a thunderbolt.

We feed on animals after their death,
I'm feared across the land,
We have no friends, only foes,
The jungle is home for us.

What am I?

Answer: Dinosaur.

Ben Sims (10)
FitzHerbert CE Primary School, Fenny Bentley

The Theme Park

People screaming on the teacup ride,
Thrill seekers deciding not to hide,
Roaring roller coasters zooming past,
Dancing dodgems darting and parking.

Candyfloss bags and cookies cooking,
Delicious Dolly Mixtures, daring to be eaten,
Chunky chips, waiting in the oven.

I love theme parks,
They are the best,
I love going on adventures,
What will happen next?

Amelia Coxon (9)
FitzHerbert CE Primary School, Fenny Bentley

Mermaid Land

In Mermaid Land,
Everything is made of sand!

They swim and play,
All of the day!

Where the sea life is happy,
No creatures are ever snappy.

Their lives would be fantastic,
If it wasn't for our plastic.

Time for us to take off our brakes,
And fix our mistakes!

Lucy Ottaway-Foster (9)
FitzHerbert CE Primary School, Fenny Bentley

Mystical World

M y mystical land

Y ou will feel spooked out

S cary, dark and gloomy,

T he mystical creatures are as magical as Christmas,

I wouldn't go there because,

C reatures will talk to you,

A nd will try to bite,

L eave, or stay, you may survive tonight!

Amy Manns-Gibson (9)
FitzHerbert CE Primary School, Fenny Bentley

Cartoon Land

I see Mickey Mouse,
Drinking the famous Grouse,
I see Donald Duck,
Covered in muck,
I see Goofy pass,
Looking as bold as brass,
I smell the lovely flowers,
And feel the sunshine showers,
I taste the summer air,
While I'm enjoying the fair.

Sam Manns-Gibson (11)
FitzHerbert CE Primary School, Fenny Bentley

Underwater Land

The sea is as blue as the sky,
The sky is as blue as the sea,
As the whales call out my name,
They squirt water out of their backs,
And the mermaids sing along,
I love the sea and the sea loves me.

Brooke Swinscoe (8)

FitzHerbert CE Primary School, Fenny Bentley

My Sweet Dream

The candy cane is sweet,
I'm ready to eat,
Pink and blue stripes,
I'm ready to bite,
With stripes so delicious,
It's so suspicious,
The flavours I taste,
My heart starts to race,
In this land where sweets grow on trees,
And candyfloss is blown on the breeze,
I imagine this place,
This colourful space,
Filled with my friends,
The fun never ends,
We'll eat and eat,
Oh what a treat,
We'll be lost in our dreams,
While eating chocolate ice creams.

Amy-Leigh Hunt (7)
Fritchley CE (A) Primary School, Fritchley

odgeball Land

You dodge the ball in Dodgeball Land.
You dip, duck, dodge and dive.
Dash around from side to side.
Find somewhere to hide.

Pick up the ball, take careful aim.
Throw it at a player.
Target animals or trees.
Earn points to win the game.

A bouncing ball might be magic.
Different rules apply.
It might explode like dynamite.
And blast you into the sky.

Oliver Toplis (7)
Fritchley CE (A) Primary School, Fritchley

Food City

F antastic food, fruit forests,

O pen the Oreo door,

O ranges grow on the green Skittles trees, with milk chocolate branches,

D elicious food houses, mine's made of sherbet.

C arefully cross the sugar-frosted candyfloss grass,

I see a wonderful world ahead,

T ogether we can explore this land,

Y ummy food for everyone!

Harriet Clarke (9)
Fritchley CE (A) Primary School, Fritchley

Minecraft Farm

Welcome to the Minecraft Farm,
Where zombies and creepers can do you harm!

Square sheep, square pigs, square cows,
It's even square how the farmer ploughs.

Wheat, beetroot and carrots all grow,
But even these are square you know!

So do come in and see what can be found,
Just remember, nothing's round!

Sam Lynam (8)
Fritchley CE (A) Primary School, Fritchley

Candy Land

I would love to live in a world of candy,
In a gingerbread house with a pet
chocolate mouse,
Outside my house there would be a great big tree,
With chocolate bark and pink candyfloss leaves,
When I look in my garden, the grass would
be green,
And it would taste just like bubblegum,
And that would be my dream.

Matilda Deans (9)
Fritchley CE (A) Primary School, Fritchley

Enchanted Forest

I went out to play, on a hot summer's day,
Who knows what I would find,
Maybe some fairies that are kind,
I looked behind some trees,
And some elves were playing with bees,
I wish I could stay,
But they had to work all day,
I stayed and watched for a while,
Then I went back with a smile.

Danielle Wade (8)
Fritchley CE (A) Primary School, Fritchley

Magic Land

M y land is magic.

A wonderful place to be.

G oing there, you will see a talking tree.

I n Magic Land there is a wishing well.

C aves have a spell which only residents can repel.

Joe Allen (8)

Fritchley CE (A) Primary School, Fritchley

Gummy Land

G iant gummy bears walking around the streets, giving people squishy hugs.

U nique lollipop trees swaying swiftly in the breeze.

M arvellous marshmallow tower standing proudly, overlooking the land.

M ajestic candyfloss unicorns gliding through the sky.

Y ummy peardrops falling from the sky and scattering on the ground.

L uscious chocolate waterfall running through the town, splashing people.

A wesome gingerbread people in their matchstick houses.

N aughty gingerbread children, playing pranks on the giant gummy bears.

D elicious treats!

Connie Abbott (11)
Howitt Primary School, Heanor

Underwater City

U nderwater City,
N othing dry, all wet,
D eadly sharks in the dark,
E els swimming all around,
R apidly darting here and there,
W ater swirling like the wind,
A lways moving, never still,
T all towers rising up above,
E verything quiet down below,
R ippling seaweed on the seabed.

C oral reef glistening
I n the clear water
T urtles floating in the waves
Y awning in the midday sun.

James Tyler (7)
Howitt Primary School, Heanor

Nightmare Land

In Nightmare Land,
Where the monsters live,
And all humans are banned.

The trees are dead,
And the rivers are red,
In this land full of dread.

As the sun rises,
And the last bell rings,
Monsters of all different sizes,
Lay back in their hiding spaces.

Tymoteusz Krzyzanowski (11)
Howitt Primary School, Heanor

Under The Mermaid Magical Ocean

I hear the waves moving and mermaids speaking
I see mermaids swimming with their pets
I smell the seaweed
I taste what mermaids eat, like edible seaweed
from the caves
I touch shells and when you put them near your
ear, you will hear the waves.

Lilly-Anne Iafrate (7)
Howitt Primary School, Heanor

Colourful Land

Your imagination will be blown away
It's out of this world
Rain is crashing down like a tornado
The bright sun blinds you
Shining down with happiness
The air mixes with the sun and makes a
beautiful rainbow.
Slide down the rainbow and splash in the
blue water
The animals are playing happily together
Would you like to see this world in Minecraft?

Theo William Stokes (8)

Larkfields Junior School, Nuthall

Ninja Rock

The sky is rocking you around
Like a wagon wheel.
The red flaming sun
Will make you special like a ninja.
A house is made out of epic emeralds.
When the sun goes down
Skeletons rise from the dead.

Aaron Curtis (10)
Larkfields Junior School, Nuthall

Mythical Chocolate Island

On my mythical chocolate island
My tummy rumbles for milk chocolate
Chocolate houses are very good to explore
Smell the sweet milk chocolate
Slide down the white chocolate hill
Chomp the crunchy road.

Thomas Wood (10)
Larkfields Junior School, Nuthall

A World Of Animals

Dogs and cats running around.
Mice making very little sound.
Blue tits flying in the sky.
Bluebirds flying oh so high.
Guinea pigs running across the floors.
Lions walking on their paws.
Monkeys swinging in the trees.
Sometimes buzzing, it's the bees.
Chameleons playing hide-and-seek.
Pelicans with their big orange beaks.
Caterpillars walking very slow.
Ants crawling down below.
Grasshoppers jumping leaf to leaf.
Fishes swimming in the Great Barrier Reef.
Butterflies moving all around us.
I hear something miaowing, it's my puss.
Come to my world, it's a beautiful view.
Do you like animals? I'm sure you do.

Ava Spencer (9)
Middleton Community Primary School, Middleton By
Wirksworth

Dark Or Light?

Dark or light, day or night
Make your choice, left or right
Flowers and sun, bats and moon
You don't know which to choose
Here, I'll make it easy for you
A splash of gold, a glimpse of blue
Good dreams is the place for you
Oh no you don't, black and grey
Bats are my birds of prey
Their eyes are sharp as an eagle's
Their wings as dark as night
They fight like the king of the jungle
They squeak their mighty roar
They make you shiver and shake
Make sure they don't come through your door!

Shannon Iris Rose Harrison

Middleton Community Primary School, Middleton By
Wirksworth

Sparkling Jewels And Golden Crowns

One day I stepped out of my front door,
But just when I thought my foot would hit the floor,
I found myself floating up and up,
Entering the world beyond

I was entering the world of sparkling jewels and golden crowns
The world where shining diamonds fall from the sky
So come to this world, don't be shy!

This world was made for me
It's the world I love
And this is where I want to be!

Hailie Croll (10)
Middleton Community Primary School, Middleton By Wirksworth

Beauty Above

No one can dance like the stars in the sky,
Or sing like the silvery moon.

Nothing's as pretty as what you see at night,
The greatest navy blue.

Forest green, fresh and new,
Flowers beautiful and colourful too.
Many others are here down below,
Houses, mountains and mistletoe.

None of which can compare,
To the beauty living right up there.
The beauty above.

Hannah Fretter (11)
Middleton Community Primary School, Middleton By
Wirksworth

The Land Under The Waves

Candy canes growing out of the ground,
Marshmallow grass all around.
Magical monuments floating in the sea,
Whilst starfish that lie there, smile with glee.

Creatures great and small live there,
But when sharks come by, other creatures
get scared.

The coral reefs act as houses,
All the creatures there wear snakeskin trousers!

Oliver Love (11)

Middleton Community Primary School, Middleton By
Wirksworth

Sparkly, Magical Unicorn Land

U nicorns, so sparkly and so magical,
N ot a dot of dark falls upon you.
I n your multicoloured world of joy,
C olours burst out from all the flowers.
O ver the gem-filled happy land,
R ainbows shine high above you.
N ow, how I wish I was there.

Breidi Megan Moran (8)
Middleton Community Primary School, Middleton By Wirksworth

In The Forest

In the forest where I lost my toys,
I saw a big scary house and heard a noise,
I went closer to the door and heard a knock,
I quickly ran as fast as I could,
And bumped into a very hard rock,
I broke my nose, it really hurt,
Out of nowhere came a man, he said,
"Nice to meet you, my name's Burt."
"Ahh!" I screamed. "You are scary."
Next thing I knew, I bumped into a fairy,
This one was mean and very hairy,
She had a moustache and beard,
I said, "You look really weird."
Her hair was a very dark, ugly green,
Her hands weren't very clean,
She had green, sticky bogies all over them,
When she coughed,
She coughed up some phlegm,
When I woke up, I realised it was a dream,
My mum came in with hot chocolate and
whipped cream!

Zaynah Khan (11)
Normanton House School, Derby

Fishy Swishy Sea!

Welcome to Fishy Swishy Sea
What a wonderful place to be
Humans breathing underwater
Everyone's filled with laughter
Dolphin rides are oh so fun
No one's fun is ever done
Sea surfing is everyone's favourite thing to do
Surfing right out in the blue
Coral climbing is the best part
It is a work of art
Seaweed sliding is the one I love
You can go up, up and above
Oh Bubble Fish you can pop, pop, pop
And nobody has to mop, mop, mop
Seashell making is so boring
Because you have to do it in the morning
Octopus' tentacles are spinning all around
But none of them touch the ground
Starfish are swimming everywhere
To grant you a wish there
Sea turtles swim in the current of the sea

Where they play and laugh with glee
Always come back to fishy swishy sea
It is truly a wonderful place to be!

Hafsa Bhatti (9)

Normanton House School, Derby

Plant World

Trees with beautiful flowers,
Which look like long towers,
On windy days they spread like showers,
It takes me hours,
To collect those clovers,
No one is allowed to have sleepovers,
All the plants are very gentle,
None of them are mental,
No one is allowed to cut trees, please!
Wood will be made out of cheese,
Though there will be many bees,
The temperature will be about 21 degrees,
So you won't freeze,
Bushes with sharp thorns,
Which are as sharp as a bull's horns,
You can have delicious sweetcorn,
So come join me!

Ayesha Ahmed (11)
Normanton House School, Derby

In Sports World...

In Sports World...

Rainbows made of balls,
The fun here really calls,
Come here and join the fun,
Run around happy in the sun,
Balls come down like rain,
If they hit you, they may cause pain,
A colourful world for you,
There's so much to do,
Whatever the weather, come and play,
Play your sports every day,
The sun's a big yellow football,
It shines on houses so tall,
Tennis, football, we have them all,
So come and play in this beautiful world,
It all happens here in Sports World.

Halimah Hussain
Normanton House School, Derby

The Magical Kingdom Of Candy

In the Kingdom Of Candy,
It's very magical,
There's sweetie treats everywhere,
Sherbet, all the colours of the rainbow,
Mixed with magical stardust,
Strawberry bonbons, sweet and cheery,
Bursting with love,
Fizzy belts full of colour,
Lead you to the rainbow,
Little Stars which shine like the sun,
In the land of cotton candy,
Everything is so fluffy,
It floats you away in your dreams,
In the Kingdom Of Candy,
It's very yummy,
There's sweetie treats everywhere.

Sumaiyah Naseer (10)
Normanton House School, Derby

Pirate World

Pirates murder just to plunder,
They shoot just to get loot,
They sail away from whales because they're fat,
So they run like rats,
Their land is filled with sand,
Their houses are dusty,
And their cannons are rusty,
Pirates' worst enemies are cats,
They wear hats to scare away rats,
Pirates' favourite food is rice,
As well as mice,
Nothing can steal the pirates' rice,
Except for the mice!

Abdul Rahman Basit (11)
Normanton House School, Derby

Football Fantasy Land

Here at Anthem City,
Arguments are solved with penalty shoot-outs,
'You'll never walk alone' is the song people shout.

Glory, glory, there's a blue moon,
At the top of the league, we'll be there soon.

Blue is the colour, football is the game,
Apples look like footballs,
Ronaldo scores and rises to fame.

Red and blue shirts, we're on your side,
Tackle, shoot, score and slide!

M Ibrahim Naseer (8)
Normanton House School, Derby

Missing Imagination Land

This is within a land of imagination that got lost
It was wild and creative
It dashed away in the bitter frost
What an imagination it was
So funny, entertaining and chilled
Nearly there, but more left to be built
Anger, sadness and joy
Sometimes it would destroy
Emotions can never be fully controlled
More future yet to be foretold
And now gone
For those who are reading, hold on
The story has just begun.

Zayan Bashir (10)
Normanton House School, Derby

Smoke City

There is a lot of smoke in this city,
But there are actually lots of things to see.

Everyone here loves smoke,
Just as some people love Coke.

If you walk down the street,
You will feel smoke against your feet.

When you go inside a house,
You will see nothing, not even a mouse.

We do have other things,
We have fun things.

We have a smoke pool,
That's pretty cool!

Ishaaq Naeem (11)
Normanton House School, Derby

Football Land

This land is the perfect place for this,
When we arrive on the pitch, we can feel the bliss,
The game will give you quite a thrill,
In summer's heat and in winter's chill,
Popping pads and pounding feet,
Will lead to our opponents' defeat,
A taste of sweat, hit after hit,
The offence and defence never quit,
Move the ball and stop the run,
Let's show our fans who's number one!

Hasan Malik (9)
Normanton House School, Derby

Aqua City!

Under the sea
There's lots to see
There's a city
And it looks very pretty
There's plenty of jewels
But not many schools!

Everyone is busy
And wants to feel fizzy
All is jolly because of the lollies
But when they eat chilli
They get all silly!

Come and visit
This part of the sea
Because it's just
For you and me!

Yusrah Khandakar (9)
Normanton House School, Derby

Candy Land

In my Candy Land I can see...
A beautifully decorated gingerbread house
I can smell peppermint scent in the air
I can feel the red, sticky strawberry laces swishing
against my legs
I can touch the soft treetops made of candyfloss
I can hear footsteps squelching in the
caramel river
I can taste the Starbursts falling from the sky
I wish I lived in Candy Land!

Musab Asir (9)
Normanton House School, Derby

Chocolate Land

Chocolate, chocolate, chocolate,
How I love eating chocolate,
When it melts, it turns all runny,
People make it into the shape of a bunny,
When frozen, it turns all hard,
When we break it, its crumbs are like
brown shards,
So tasty and so yummy,
It will always be a favourite in my tummy,
Chocolate, chocolate, chocolate,
How I love eating chocolate!

Muhammad Umar Hussain (11)

Normanton House School, Derby

My Lollipop Land!

My lollipop land is the best,
Better than all the rest,
My lollies are so sweet,
Such a scrumptious treat,
I lick them all day and night,
Such a wonderful, wonderful sight,
My lollipops glisten when it's light,
And look pretty in the twilight,
The spirals and swirls have an incredible taste,
Making the town children grab them with haste.

Hafsa Bint-Umran (8)
Normanton House School, Derby

Criminolia

In Criminolia your destiny is to steal
Life over there isn't very real
Criminals here, criminals there
Someone might even grab your underwear!
There is no nature that is green
Even the animals are very mean
The shopping place isn't very grand
So don't come to this dreaded land
For gold is the only thing that they demand.

Hassan Mahmood (10)
Normanton House School, Derby

Forever Friends

F riends are fun and forever keeping,
R unning about and laughing,
I care about them and you should too,
E xcited about the day to come,
N ew friends are silver, old friends are gold,
D on't mess with me or my friends
S uper, silly and smiley are my friends'
personalities.

Ayisha Halima Qureshi (11)
Normanton House School, Derby

Candy World

Candy World, Candy World,
Everything's pretty,
In Candy World,
Everything is made out of sweets,
Nothing is made from wheat.

Everything is delicious,
Nothing there is suspicious.

When you're angry,
Eat some candy.

Come and visit this place,
So you can fill your belly!

M Ahmed Ahmed (9)
Normanton House School, Derby

Magic Land

In Magic Land,
There's a waving wand,
That makes the spells,
From flying books to magic bells,
Or magic jewellery that you could sell,
Flying tents roam the air,
Which creates the scene of a magic fair,
People fly from across the sand,
To come and see my magical land!

Noor Hussain
Normanton House School, Derby

Candy Land

Candy, candy,
Candy is delicious
It isn't suspicious
In my land
The candy canes are trees
Take a lick and you'll eat them all
They grow every year
And you can hear
Skittles fall
Catch one in your mouth
You'll eat it all!

Uzair Abid (8)
Normanton House School, Derby

Rich And Happy Forever

My land is cool
People happy
People rich
Beautiful flowers
Diamonds and gold
Shiny as the sun
People explore
Looking for treasure
Every day
Will you come?
There's lots to do!

Hamza Mahmood (7)
Normanton House School, Derby

My Hotel

As I walked through the dead of night
I gazed into oblivion; empty was the world.
Like a ballerina, I calmly spun around
and to my astonishment, a flickering light,
disappearing and reappearing
as what looked like figures strolled past the
source.
When I drew nearer, blocks came into view.
And when the picture was completed,
in front of me was a hotel... a big one!
Red carpets, chandeliers and flowers adorned the
room,
A fragrance of 'blockioli' filled the room,
The sound of a 'blockestra' drifted through the
room.
Warmth was in the room,
a room that I'd created:
a heaven in a three dimensional existence
until I was called for tea.
And when my brother entered this land
My hotel was no more...
"Arthur!"

Madeleine Bambridge (11)
North Wheatley Primary School, South Wheatley

The Island

Open your eyes
What do you see?
A land of wonder and mystery
The rich turquoise ocean arrives
On the shores of a lush emerald island
But how can this be?
It's a cold Arctic space
Surely nothing can grow in such a desolate place?

But there is life lurking in the depths
Murderous creatures guard this bewitching place
No one shall pass, they need to defend
But why?

Untouched, unspoilt, hidden from view
Mythical winged giants,
Swaying green palm trees laden with fruit
Silver flowing waterfalls, crystal caves
The wonders of life, they want to remain
For if man touches the land and spreads pollution
There will be no beauty and no solution.

Callum Dale (10)
North Wheatley Primary School, South Wheatley

If Minecraft Was Food

If Minecraft was food,
It would have candy cane trees,
Sugary candyfloss for the leaves,
The candyfloss sheep would graze on the grass,
And peppermint pigs would shine brightly
like glass.

If Minecraft was food,
It would have gummy bunnies,
And every day would be bright and sunny,
But when it rained, the puddles would be milk,
Flavoured like chocolate, smooth as silk.

If Minecraft was food,
It would have caramel waterfalls,
Underneath, a liquorice spider crawls,
And the dirt would be cake underfoot,
Under that is where the toffee stone would be put.

If Minecraft was food,
We would wish it was real,

And we would wonder how it would feel,
If Minecraft was the truth,
In our ever-shortening youth.

Freya Rose North (11)
North Wheatley Primary School, South Wheatley

The Great Railway Street

R ailway Street starts near a theatre in Newcastle North Dock

A t the start of the street, there is a small country station, but unlike other streets, it has a glass roof

I n the centre of this unique street, there is a café named 'The Buffet Car'

L ook at the grand Paddington statue, that is made of marble, tempting people to take pictures

W hat was that banging noise? It's the train depot workers on a train that could change the world!

A s the street turns into an impressive terminus, the gift shop gives free souvenirs

Y our tour ends here.

Dominic Newby (9)

North Wheatley Primary School, South Wheatley

Football Fever Land

F un and fast in Football Land, the players run
O ut onto the muddy grass
O ver the line
T o player number nine, the
B linding ball bounces in the back of the net
A ll the crowd cheer
L isten, is it a goal?
L et the referee decide, the whistle blows.

F antastic!
E ach player has his part in their team's
V ictory!
E ach one has a brave heart
R eady to play their next part.

Owen Dale (10)
North Wheatley Primary School, South Wheatley

My Land

It's a fine place with lots of honey,
But not much money,
Sometimes we need to weed,
So that the animals can feed,
We run every day,
To keep the fat away,
We open the door,
And obey the law,
We like coffee,
But hate toffee,
We like peas,
But not bees,
And we smell of cheese,
We have good looks,
And lots of books,
We've got some cake,
But not much steak!

Scarlett Wilkinson (9)
North Wheatley Primary School, South Wheatley

Birthday Land

B irthdays are full of celebration and fun,
I magine what you could do in my new world, there is lots to be done,
R ibbons fall from the sky,
T his time you'll wish it could rain all the time,
H ow much fun would it be...
D ancing and eating cake all day, without a worry?
A ll the fun things to be done,
Y ou'll have to see, how about you come along?

Neve Lily Baker (11)
North Wheatley Primary School, South Wheatley

I Can...

I can craft my favourite sports stadium,
I can build something without no one stopping me,
I can create snowy mountains anywhere,
I can shape a boat to sail,
I can see creatures that I have never seen before,
I can explore my world and everything in it,
I can develop my life through Minecraft,
Everything is possible when I am a child
in Minecraft.

Ben Launders (10)
North Wheatley Primary School, South Wheatley

Book World

Open a book
And I'm sure you will find
Characters and places of many kinds

Open a book
And turn the page and see if you're in
A train, a car or a plane

Open a book
And you could be, a fairy, a monster
Or even just me

Open a book
Just as I might, do
You read me, just as I've read you?

Nicole Marie Cocksedge (11)
North Wheatley Primary School, South Wheatley

The Enchanted Forest

In the Enchanted Forest,
It is an unusual place,
As it moves to different spaces,
With disappearing trees,
The leaves die away.

All the creatures are magical,
There are thought to be pixies, some say,
Some day you shall see it,
But remember, it will fade away!

Katie McKay (10)
North Wheatley Primary School, South Wheatley

The Magical World Of Hogwarts

The magical castle is far away,
With witches and wizards galore,
Peeves the poltergeist, ready to pounce,
Hides behind every door.

Harry, Ron and Hermione too,
Get there by Hogwarts Express,
Soon the castle will come into view,
Time to clean up their mess.

Ella Worden (10)
North Wheatley Primary School, South Wheatley

Unicorn Land

U nique, this world certainly is.

N o nightmares allowed.

I nside this world, you will be safe.

C ones full of ice cream.

O ver the rainbow you will find treasure.

R ain never comes to this land.

N o dreams are forgotten.

Ruby Coco Brailich (9)

S. Anselm's School, Bakewell

Dream Land

D readed unicorns who take over the land
R ainbows are all over
E vil door that leads to death
A nimals that are kind and can talk
M y world is created with dreams
S weets to make the unicorns hyper.

Holly Kilner (9)
S. Anselm's School, Bakewell

Candy Land

C urious animals roam the land

A nimals eat all the tasty treats

N o dreams are forgotten here

D inosaurs stuff their faces with ice cream

Y ou won't regret living in this world!

Isabella Mayson (9)

S. Anselm's School, Bakewell

Gravity

In the depths of space
At a faraway place

The moon orbits the Earth
Shooting stars give birth

Spectacular colours we see through a telescope
Planets being discovered gives us more hope

An interesting topic
We have to travel on a rocket

The phase of the moon affects our moods

When we see our beautiful setting sun
We know our day is done!

5, 4, 3, 2, 1... Blast-off!

Isabelle Bowen (10)
Southglade Primary School, Bestwood Park

Dinosaur Land

D inosaurs
I ndividual
N o one likes them
O ne dinosaur still lives
S tegosaurus
A lone in Russia
U p high and far away
R oaring in all directions

Dinosaurs live
They like to shift
They like to eat
They have mega feet!

Damian Raynor (10)
Southglade Primary School, Bestwood Park

Candy Magic Land

The crocodiles are made of fizzy Coca-Cola in the chocolate river.
The birds are made of gooey candyfloss and flap their fizzy strawberry-laced wings.
The fish are blowing bubblegum while eating the chocolate river.
The mushrooms are chocolate and inside is whipped cream.
Skittles are the path in the chocolate forest.
Chocolate chips are the branches.
There's one massive ice cream hill.
Gingerbread men walk on the marshmallow crocodiles.
Dragons roar chocolate fire.
Lollipops swirl around the chocolate fountain.

Welcome to Candy Magic Land!

Alexis Summer Bode (8)
St Edward's Catholic Academy, Swadlincote

Lego Candyland

Five friends went on holiday,
but the plane went the wrong way.
They went down instead of up.
They landed in a chocolate cup.

They were in Lego Candyland,
With emojis, it was grand.
Then the Lego ninja candy unicorn said,
"Where are we and what's in my head?"

Candyland smells of yummy sweets,
And filled with the yummiest of treats.
You can see up high.
Candy birds in the sky.
Edible Lego candy.
And the rapping pig, Randy.
I enjoyed my visit.
It was exquisite.

Ruby Carpenter (8)

St Edward's Catholic Academy, Swadlincote

The World Of Candy

In my lane
Everything is made from candy cane
And when you come, you will find
There are gummy phones, a PS4, everything you
can imagine and more
And if you eat them, you will be full to your core.
The castle is the heart of this land
And in there we have a candy band
They play night and day
Their songs are about candy and sweets
Come along and join in singing and give them
a hand
The King and Queen of Candy Cane Lane
Say brush your teeth night and day
This will help to fight tooth decay!

Ethan Hanif Edmonds (9)
St Edward's Catholic Academy, Swadlincote

Magical Land

Magical Land looks like a place you see in
your dreams
Rainbow unicorns, candy penguins and
gummy glory
Magical Land smells like a candy store
With candyfloss chairs and Starburst tables
Magical Land tastes like the sweetest and sourest
thing in your galaxy
Magical Land feels like a marshmallow pillow with
a candyfloss blanket
Magical Land sounds like the most thrilling thing
on Earth
Where grand unicorns lead the dancing.

Lilly Cox (8)
St Edward's Catholic Academy, Swadlincote

Candy Magic Land

A land far away
A place where dreams come true
Clouds like candyfloss
Everywhere, lollipop trees
Birds sitting on chocolate sticks
Marshmallow crocodiles floating in the
chocolate river

Birds blowing bubblegum, popping bubbles
Ice cream hills
Gingerbread men living in a gingerbread house
Marshmallow crashing into melted chocolate
I don't like marshmallow, I like candy!

Megan Rose Coope (9)
St Edward's Catholic Academy, Swadlincote

Dead Ender HQ

In the land of gaming
Without any blaming
Was the Dead Ender HQ
With all the food to chew
Couldn't even rest
With every single quest
Everything here is so fair
Break the rules, don't dare
If you want to hack
Don't use the jet pack
Though you can fly
With candy pie
Everything you see
Will give you glee
Come and join us
We are not far away.

Evan Shipley (9)
St Edward's Catholic Academy, Swadlincote

The Dream World

There is a world called Dead Enders HQ
There is enough food but not much to chew!
There's gaming and blaming
But you never break a sweat
There's coding and exploding
You'll never lose a bet
When you hack, you'll get a jet pack
There's a lot of simulators that you can create
So you should go, it's not far away
Bring your friends
Come and play!

Sonnie Mercer (8)
St Edward's Catholic Academy, Swadlincote

Football Land

I was entered for the World Cup,
As happy as can be,
I played for Portugal,
The best country.

I was entered for the World Cup,
Hoping we would win,
There were other great players,
But I was the best.

I was entered for the World Cup,
In Russia it was based,
Other countries were trying to win,
But I put them in the bin.

Jack Freeman (9)
St Edward's Catholic Academy, Swadlincote

The World Of Chocolate And Candy

There are candy cane trees
There are Smartie leaves
There are chocolate roofs
There are chocolate roads

There are Gummy Bear women
There are Haribo men
There is a chocolate fountain
There is a chocolate mountain

There are gingerbread houses
There are roads made of toffee
There is a plane
That goes to Candy Cane Lane!

Autumn Warner (9)
St Edward's Catholic Academy, Swadlincote

Magical Land

Magical Land looks like one of your dreams
coming true
This magical place smells like marshmallows being
toasted
Magical Land tastes like the greatest thing you've
ever had
Just take a lick of the candy canes, candyfloss
and more
This magical place feels like it has a
candyfloss ground
Magical Land is the place to visit.

Isabel Meikle (9)
St Edward's Catholic Academy, Swadlincote

The World Of Candy

In my street, I saw a treat,
I saw a lot of Smarties leaves,
I went into my gingerbread house,
The PS4 tasted like strawberry,
The TV screen was toffee,
The Rubix cube was made out of chocolate,
The phones were made out of gummies,
The people were made out of marshmallows,
The babies were mini marshmallows.

Keenan Baldwin (9)
St Edward's Catholic Academy, Swadlincote

Lego Chocolate River

Lego chocolate river, so fast and vast
During the warm weather it goes all sloppy
During the icy weather it is all frozen
It's the one that's chosen
Always flowing in the air, never blowing
It's dark chocolate, but it flows like a normal river
So it should be declared a normal river
But chocolatey!

Ethan Kelly (9)
St Edward's Catholic Academy, Swadlincote

The World Cup 2018

I entered the World Cup,
As lucky as I can be,
I played for Portugal,
Trying to defeat Russia.

I entered the World Cup,
Knowing we would win,
And when we play a team,
I'll put them in the beaten bin.

I entered the World Cup,
We were in the final,
I hope we win,
And we do!

Sam Sellers (9)
St Edward's Catholic Academy, Swadlincote

Slime Land

Slime Land looks like a boggy, gloomy place
Stretchy, sticky, gooey and moist
With a green glittery sky and a mountain full
of slime
A fun land to play in and a fun place to build in
It looks like a blast for mess makers
It is not edible, it is not smelly
So don't let it go down your belly!

Gabriella Jane Bellafronte (9)
St Edward's Catholic Academy, Swadlincote

Candy Land

C andy Land
A lot of rainbow colours
N ice waterfall that has candy rocks
D own flows the Lego lava
Y um yum!

L ooks like a rainbow
A house made out of Lego sweets
N ice candy canes and lollipops
D elicious chocolate trees.

Isabelle-Mollie Flanagan-Nicholls (9)
St Edward's Catholic Academy, Swadlincote

A Trip To The Moon

Dog Planet was its name,
There once lived a dog called Sage,
All his life he wanted to,
Fly up to the moon,
When his 30th birthday came,
He went to the moon,
Like in a video game,
In space he saw a magic case,
But then he got chased,
So he went to space no more.

George Alexander Radley (9)
St Edward's Catholic Academy, Swadlincote

Unicorn And Stitch Land

Unicorn and Stitch Land is where your dreams
come true,
Even unicorns might say boo!
The sun is a lollipop with a unicorn horn,
Houses are made of chocolate,
With dressed up unicorns that make you laugh,
A glittery rainbow river,
Unicorn and Stitch floats too.

Connie Denning (8)

St Edward's Catholic Academy, Swadlincote

Candy Magic Land

Candy Land is a place where dreams come true
You can take a chocolate bubble blowing
bird's nest
And suck it up like a bowl of spaghetti
Candy Land is a place where a beautiful chocolate
river flows
You can take a walk into the gigantic
candyfloss forest.

Myles Mondesir (8)
St Edward's Catholic Academy, Swadlincote

Candy Land

C andy Land
A lot of candy
N ice candyfloss
D elicious chocolate
Y um yum

L and of lollipops
A nd candy chocolate
N ice smell of strawberry milkshake
D elicious rainbow colours.

Cerise Joyce Cotton (8)
St Edward's Catholic Academy, Swadlincote

Slimeville

The candyfloss is the fluff,
The world is about to puff,
All the trees are falling,
Oh this might be appalling!
The rain goo is so tough,
It always makes me rough,
There's so much slime,
I don't have the time,
To finish this rhyme!

Amelie Lewek (8)
St Edward's Catholic Academy, Swadlincote

Dog Planet

Dog Planet is a dog and a planet,
Dog Planet is a colourful place,
Dog Planet gives you a happy face,
Dog Planet has a new dog city,
The dogs are very wise,
Dog Planet doesn't have bad guys!

Domink Sidorczuk (9)
St Edward's Catholic Academy, Swadlincote

Unicorn And Stitch Land

The river is a sparkling rainbow
The unicorn's fur is sparkling
Stitch is hard to find
He blends into the walls
The walls are made of chocolate
It always grows back.

Lewis Rayson (8)

St Edward's Catholic Academy, Swadlincote

Slime Land

Slime Land feels gooey, sticky and smooth
Slime Land sounds magical and fun
Slime Land looks like a bath of slime
Slime Land tastes like rotten meat
Slime Land smells horrid!

Aimee-Leigh Maisie Randle (9)
St Edward's Catholic Academy, Swadlincote

The Best Dream I've Ever Had

I once dreamed of a place
That was totally, utterly ace
It had candy cane trees
And gum making bees
It was officially the most supreme place!

Evangelene Puthussery (9)
St Edward's Catholic Academy, Swadlincote

Fairy Land

M any things live here,
A mazing things too,
G ot to come here,
I can't wait!
C oolest place ever is where we are going!

W hat are we waiting for?
A wesome unicorns are waiting,
N o bad people allowed,
D ogs that are magically, magnificently mad,
S uper funny fairies fly.

F antastic fairies,
O r Pegasus the flying cat,
R eally, this is all true!

Y ellow dogs do magic practise,
O rca the fairy queen too,
U h, I need some rest!

Eva Brailsford (8)
St Giles CE Primary School, Matlock

Animal World

In the land where lions roar,
Where big bears snore,
I can't ask for anymore,
Where snow leopards leap,
Where hedgehogs sleep,
I wonder what animal I want to keep.

Where horses run,
It's so much fun,
Not a glimpse of a nun,
Where dogs bark,
There are signs of a lark,
And a giraffe called Mark.

Where rabbits jump,
They have a tail like a fluffy bump,
Where birds fly,
Actually I,
Would like to see a parrot lie.

Where bugs crawl,
And sometimes fall,
Where bees sting,

There isn't a bee king,
And the stinging noise is 'ping!'

It's the Animal World!

Maisey Diveney-Moffat (8)
St Giles CE Primary School, Matlock

Candy Land

I love sweets,
I can hear the birds' tweets,
In a land where candy lives,
Where people eat sweets, definitely kids.

There are peppermint candy canes,
A lot of lanes of sweets,
And ice cream snow,
Lots of candy bows.

A big chocolate cake,
For you to bake,
Some candy fruit limes,
And edible slime.

I don't know what's wrong with me,
I need a sweet cup of tea,
I need a sweet,
And a bird to tweet.

With all this candy,
My mouth is tangy,

I need a rest,
And a candy test.

I need a candy dinner,
Always a winner,
A candy book,
Just take a look.

Emily Kerry (9)
St Giles CE Primary School, Matlock

Candy Disco!

C andy everywhere, gummy bears and
   gingerbread people,
A disco I can hear,
N ed and Nora are here and Bob and Boblina,
D airy Milk chocolate lake, it's amazing,
Y ummy, gummy dance floor, colourful and
   bouncy.

L ovely gingerbread house with a candy cane
   floor,
A tree trunk that's chocolate with candyfloss on
   top,
N ed and Nora dancing on the colourful dance
   floor,
D ancing Gummy Bears Bob and Boblina having
   fun.

Lila Staley (8)
St Giles CE Primary School, Matlock

Candy Land

C hocolate ducks floating
A round in the chocolate river
N ice Skittles and Smarties on a glitter rainbow
D affodils blooming in the bright sun
Y ummy marshmallows to sit on and eat a
chocolate picnic

L ovely animals drinking from the chocolate
stream
A nimals being born
N ow I have animals around me, giving me sweets
D aisies are everywhere and are edible too.

Daisy Bridger (7)
St Giles CE Primary School, Matlock

Candy Land

C andyfloss bushes,
A nd people made of gingerbread,
N aturally marshmallow is drizzled in chocolate,
D oors made of candyfloss,
Y ellow banana-flavoured lollipops.

L ovely bubblegum mountains, high and tall,
A lso sour apple tasting grass,
N ow you can taste the gingerbread,
D ancing gingerbread people.

I love Candy Land

Sienna Gulliford (8)
St Giles CE Primary School, Matlock

Music Land

M y lovely land loves dancing,
U se all different types of melody to rock,
S winging around like a disco ball,
I love glitter and jewels and I love my dress,
C an I come next time please?

L ovely colours: gold, silver, blue and black,
A mazing snacks,
N ow the speakers say, 'Little Mix'
D efinitely, I'm coming again!

Hannah Katherine Smith (7)
St Giles CE Primary School, Matlock

Zoo Kingdom

Z ebras running fast to the water,
O striches drinking from the river,
O range iguanas.

K angaroo hopped up to the horse,
I n the water the penguins swam,
N elly the elephant was huge,
G iraffes have tall necks,
D eep underground there was a monkey,
O ctopus with big, long tentacles,
M ice scuttled up the pipes.

Andrew Slater (8)
St Giles CE Primary School, Matlock

Nightmare Land

N ight is scary,

I t's when scary killer clowns come at night,

G hosts swim around at night,

H owever, Ender dragons fire at you,

T ill midnight, there are zombies,

M ad skeletons shooting arrows,

A t 3 o'clock, Candy Man is coming for you,

R arely, Slender Man is killing you,

E ating blood, yuck! Yuck! Yuck!

Ellis Mousley (8)
St Giles CE Primary School, Matlock

Dinosaur Land

Dinosaurs are scary,
Dinosaurs are fat,
Dinosaurs are big,
They have blood-covered teeth as well.

Dinosaurs are different,
Dinosaurs have sharp claws,
Dinosaurs are fierce,
Dinosaurs can eat you up in one go.

Dinosaurs are terrifying,
Dinosaurs are everywhere,
Beware the dinosaurs,
They're coming to get you.

Dinosaurs roar!

Jayleize Scoffins (9)
St Giles CE Primary School, Matlock

Nightmare

N ight comes, zombies too,

I can hear the owls,

G hosts float in the air,

H orrible ghosts eating your brains,

T oes, hairy toes poking out of the bin,

M y dream is getting worse and worse,

A nd goosebumps up my arms,

R ats running to bite the reindeer,

E verything is frightening.

Jackell Scoffins (8)
St Giles CE Primary School, Matlock

Dream Land

D reams are like magic movies,
R olls and beautiful swirls in the bright sky,
E verywhere there are fluffy unicorns,
A ll the land is covered in beautiful animals,
M any animals live here in my world.

Dreams are awesome!

Jolie Haywood (8)
St Giles CE Primary School, Matlock

Pirate World

P irates zoom around everywhere,
I n their speedy vessels,
R ocketing to the horizon, they
A re ready,
T o plunder rich ships,
E ating horrible hard biscuits, they could,
S top and get some better food.

Michael Gibson (9)
St Giles CE Primary School, Matlock

Dream Land

D reams feel as if you are floating in the air,
R acing, rushing around,
E agles and awesome, amazing bunnies,
A ir filled with flying edible houses,
M agic unicorns in the clouds.

I love dreams!

Summer Oldfield (7)

St Giles CE Primary School, Matlock

Dinosaur World

I can hear dinosaurs eating plants,
I can see fierce dinosaurs eating meat,
I can smell flesh from the herbivores,
I can taste the sweet water,
I can touch a dinosaur called a brontosaurus

I love dinosaurs!

Aidan Woodward (7)
St Giles CE Primary School, Matlock

Chocolate Wood

C hocolate is so tasty,
H ot chocolate melted pool,
O h, you ate your way out,
C hocolate Wood is like Hollywood,
O ff road, it will melt you down,
L ots of fun,
A car is melting in the sun,
T he sun will melt you, keep out!
E at too much, you will be sick,

W here is the chocolate?
O r an ice cream,
O r a tasty snack,
D on't eat it all!

John-Phil Cunningham (9)
St Luke's CE Primary School, Shireoaks

Football Village

In Football Village, it's goaltastic,
There's loads of matches to tear up patches,
It's not pretty, but beautiful,
The goals are extraordinary, not ordinary,
Amazing places you'll want to see,
So come learn more with me,
There's chanting and dancing,
So visit Football Village.

Nina Davide (8)
St Luke's CE Primary School, Shireoaks

Dangerous Creatures

D angerous creatures are still out there,
R ipping people to death,
A tooth is as sharp as a knife,
G rabbing you and hurting you,
O h no! The dragons are invading the land,
N ibbling on people's hearts and ruling Earth,
S neaking up on you every second.

Sophie Robley (9)
St Luke's CE Primary School, Shireoaks

Tyler The Tiger

Tigers are cool
They swim in a pool
Tyler lives in a candy forest
The candy is dandy
Tyler the tiger
Has a rider.

But all the bats
And also the rats
Had eaten all the candy
Which wasn't dandy
But overnight
It grew back.

Ava Keyworth (8)
St Luke's CE Primary School, Shireoaks

Skittles Land

S kittles are candy
K ids are getting ready to stuff their faces
I love Skittles
T asty treats
T angy tongues
L ick your lips
E at until you're sick
S till eating!

Finlay McEvoy (8)
St Luke's CE Primary School, Shireoaks

The Race

There is a race in Heaven against Dark Place
All the animals are tremendously tough
In Dark Place, they are as rude as rhinos
But in Heaven, they are as kind as a bee.

Devan Singh Gill (8)
St Luke's CE Primary School, Shireoaks

Candy Dog Land

C andy is nice

A nimals are made out of it here

N erf guns are here to play with

D ogs can play too

Y ellow candy sun glows.

Iona Watson (8)

St Luke's CE Primary School, Shireoaks

River Land

Two little ducks quacking quickly
Through the fast flowing water
As a little girl passes by
Skipping in the water
She finds a box of treasure.

Millie Grace Pickering (8)
St Luke's CE Primary School, Shireoaks

A Mythical River

Nature,
Quiet, beautiful
You can paddle, row and walk around in it,
Like a pond, but bigger and sometimes mythical,
A mythical river!

Jessica Kate Harrison (9)
St Luke's CE Primary School, Shireoaks

Dog's Land

Dogs play in the field
Because they have fun
They play with their toys
And bark out loud.

Abbi Hopkinson (8)
St Luke's CE Primary School, Shireoaks

Treat Land

Welcome to the wonderful world of sweets,
Where you can enjoy delicious treats,
Have a swim in the M&M's waterfall,
Or eat a yummy biscuit ball.

Play baseball with a chocolate flake,
Or swim around a milkshake lake,
Climb the lollipop trees,
And hear the liquorice bees.

All of the candyfloss is blue,
Believe me, it's true,
Come and visit this land,
Then you will understand.

Cameron Watkins (11)
The Linnet Independent Learning Centre, Castle Gresley

The Nightmare Realm

Oh this land is such a nightmare
Enter if you dare
Look, don't stare
You may not glare

First up you'll see a crazy clown
That wears a frown
You can walk into the town
And everyone will look down!

Ryan Elliott (11)
The Linnet Independent Learning Centre, Castle Gresley

Magical World

The Magical World is bright,
Where the stars shimmer at night.

Open your eyes and you will see,
Fairies with glitter, in the place where it it bitter.

Magical moon, glowing brightly,
It could fade but it's not very likely.

Mean witch coming along,
Leaving behind a nasty pong!

The book of bad magic is with her as well,
So hold your breath, otherwise you will smell.

Nothing is left but the witch,
Be careful, she is nothing but a snitch!

Nicole Batchford (9)
Wessington Primary School, Wessington

Candyland

C andyland has lots of streets

A nd sells the most amazing sweets

N obody dislikes these sweets

D aydreaming next to the most magical treats

Y ou can taste these wondrous flavours

L ike strawberry, vanilla, they're ever so famous

A t Candyland it is very nice

N ear Christmas it's covered in bits of frosting ice

D ecide which flavour you will have tonight.

Archie Taylor (8)

Wessington Primary School, Wessington

Dream Land

In Dream Land, a pillow is as soft as a piece
of wool.
You go to sleep and wake up in a magical world.
One of them is the magical mermaid world.
When you go to a land, your bed will go *boom!*
You will still be on that silky, soft pillow.
Dream Land is a bed of dreams.
It could be a land of chocolates and sweets.
When it's sunset, you go back to it again.

Summer Edge
Wessington Primary School, Wessington

Tropical Land

You wake up here to the enchanting songs of
the birds,
Just take a dip in the shimmering waters,
You will find yourself in a deep, dark cave,
Then jump out and watch the twilight,
Go surfing with the killer whales, if you dare,
At the end of the day, run down to the water,
Watch it topple and turn,
The water waves goodbye,
The birds sing goodnight.

Eden Kunica (8)
Wessington Primary School, Wessington

Happy Land

In Happy Land there's time to play,
Let's go and have some fun today,
There's candy trees, with some bees,
There's something magical, a flying pig,
But beware, you cannot dig!
There's a farm,
It has a barn,
There's a chocolate river,
You can swim in.
There's fast cars too,
My favourite is a Vauxhall Maloo!

Sam Brown (8)
Wessington Primary School, Wessington

Beneath The Waves

Whale song echoing in the endless blue
If you dive deep enough, there's a surprise in store
for you
Fish scales gleaming in the sunlight
Did I tell you about the sea pirates?
They're not very bright
And once every five years
There's a wonderful melody
I don't know if Max the merman could play it...
Could he?

Jasper Marshall (9)
Wessington Primary School, Wessington

Chocolate Land

In my land
It doesn't cost a grand
People say it's crazy
So if you're lazy
Come and eat
Your favourite treat
In this crazy land.

Don't be shy
There's not one fly
It all tastes good
Not a speck of wood
So come and explore
So much more
In this crazy land.

Eleanor Hayes (8)
Wessington Primary School, Wessington

My Christmas World

S anta delivers presents in my world
N aughty elves make them and
O h the tasty candy cane trees!
W inter is my magical world
B ells ring and children play
A little light sparkling in the window
L ittle snowflakes falling
L ittle lights twinkling.

Amber-Louise Buckely (9)
Wessington Primary School, Wessington

Candy City

At night, on a tight corner
I saw a bright door
I went into a new world
It was Candy City
It was all pretty
No bricks, just candy
A flying Whispa came out
Of the candyfloss clouds
Kids ate the part that
Turned into a chocolate river
A gummy snake slithered.

Oliver Davis (8)
Wessington Primary School, Wessington

My Lovely World

I have a home to fit everyone in,
It has never-ending food,
I will let anyone come in my home,
It has one hundred floors,
I will keep the house clean,
It can never be too big,
I will share everything,
You can count on me.

Louis McPherson (9)
Wessington Primary School, Wessington

Candy Block World

In Candy Block World it's so tasty,
Chocolates hanging from the tree
Do not eat them, they are all for me!
I am the candy eating king
All the candy is very yummy
You can't have any
It's in my tummy!

William Race Beckett (7)

Wessington Primary School, Wessington

Candy Land

C all everyone you know and tell them about this place,
A nd enjoy the wondrous smells that fill the air,
N ow reach up and taste the trees,
D o taste the grass that's growing there,
Y ou can even taste the ocean breeze.

L emonade rivers flowing by,
A nd candyfloss clouds up in the sky,
N ow try these petals made of strawberry lace,
D o come quick so you can stuff your face!

Freya Lilian Wilson (8)
Wirksworth Junior School, Wirksworth

Snow And Ice City

There was a snowman called Dice,
He was always as hard as ice,
Unfortunately, on a very hot day,
He melted straight away,
But he still liked tiny brown mice.

His snowman friend called Pretty Polly,
Well, she was always very jolly,
Because she was still as hard as ice,
She could still eat lots of brown mice,
And that's the thing Dice didn't like about Polly!

Lyla Hunt (8)
Wirksworth Junior School, Wirksworth

Dolphins

D ancing gracefully through the sea.

O range sunshine brightly shining on them.

L istening carefully and hearing their song.

P eacefully gliding through the sea.

H appily swimming with the colourful coral.

I n the bright blue, breezy sea they swim.

N othing could be better than a dolphin's life.

S wimming in the deep blue sea.

Caitlin Butler (7)
Wirksworth Junior School, Wirksworth

Food Land

F ood is marvellous and cool
O ver the hills is Food Land that rules
O uch! Hot chillies sting
D on't taste them.

L ick, lick, lick, I love the fresh, sweet taste of
lollies that are as sweet as apples
A pples, I love the taste of them
N utrients in fish like salmon
D oughnuts with eggs, *mmmm!*

Alyssa Briony Stone (7)
Wirksworth Junior School, Wirksworth

Gingerbread City

G ames and food is what we like,

I n the sun, we ride our bikes,

N obody gets left behind,

G ingerbread is what we eat,

E njoy your time,

R eady to play?

B ouncy castles, we have lots,

R eally excited to play?

E xcellent, let's go,

A nd don't forget,

D ogs are allowed.

Gabrielle Stocks (9)
Wirksworth Junior School, Wirksworth

Monster Valley

M y land is called Monster Valley

O pen and wild

N o humans allowed

S tory-like and fun

T he most wonderful place ever

E njoyable and exciting

R ummage around and you will find fun.

Aelita Valentina Olive Ivy Williams (8)
Wirksworth Junior School, Wirksworth

Candy Land

C andy Land is a handy land.

A land of sweets and treats.

N ice smelling treats, good to eat.

D elicious lollipop treats.

Y ou can't wait to eat.

Henry Matkin (8)
Wirksworth Junior School, Wirksworth

YoungWriters
Est. 1991

YOUNG WRITERS INFORMATION

We hope you have enjoyed reading this book – and that you will continue to in the coming years.

If you're a young writer who enjoys reading and creative writing, or the parent of an enthusiastic poet or story writer, do visit our website **www.youngwriters.co.uk**. Here you will find free competitions, workshops and games, as well as recommended reads, a poetry glossary and our blog.

If you would like to order further copies of this book, or any of our other titles, then please give us a call or visit **www.youngwriters.co.uk**.

Young Writers
Remus House
Coltsfoot Drive
Peterborough
PE2 9BF
(01733) 890066
info@youngwriters.co.uk